the it girl's
guide to video

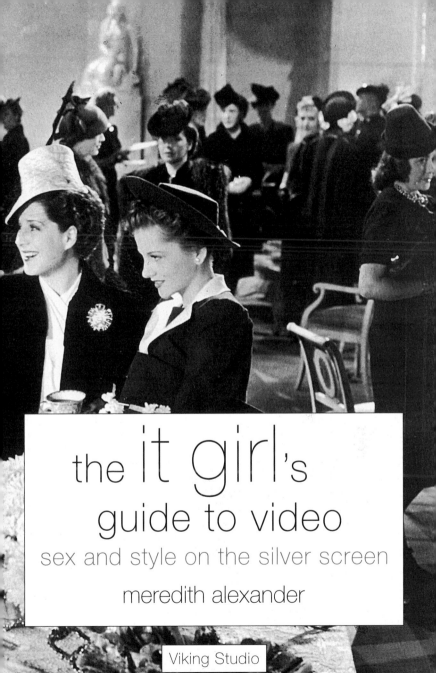

the it girl's
guide to video
sex and style on the silver screen

meredith alexander

Viking Studio

Page 1: Doris Day keeps her reputation squeaky clean in *Pillow Talk*, 1959.

Pages 2–3: Phyllis Povah, Rosalind Russell, Norma Shearer, and Joan Fontaine dish the dirt over tea and crumpets in *The Women*, 1939.

VIKING STUDIO
Published by the Penguin Group
Penguin Putnam Inc., 375 Hudson Street,
New York, New York 10014, U.S.A.
Penguin Books Ltd, 27 Wrights Lane,
London W8 5TZ, England
Penguin Books Australia Ltd, Ringwood,
Victoria, Australia
Penguin Books Canada Ltd, 10 Alcorn Avenue,
Toronto, Ontario, Canada M4V 3B2
Penguin Books (N.Z.) Ltd, 182–190 Wairau Road,
Auckland 10, New Zealand

Penguin Books Ltd, Registered Offices:
Harmondsworth, Middlesex, England

First published by Viking Studio 1999

1 3 5 7 9 10 8 6 4 2

Photographs reproduced by permission of Archive Photos.
Credits: Darlene Hammond/Archive Photos, 91; Joel Kudler/Archive Photos,
2–3, 76; Metro-Goldwyn-Mayer/Archive Photos, 61; Paramount
Pictures/Archive Photos, 39, 70; Popperfoto, 72, 96; RKO Radio/Archive
Photos, 69; Universal Pictures/Archive Photos, 115.

Library of Congress Cataloging-in-Publication Data

Alexander, Meredith.
The it girl's guide to video : sex and style on the silver screen /
Meredith Alexander.
p.   cm.
Includes indexes.
ISBN 0-14-028594-6
1. Motion pictures for women. 2. Motion pictures—Catalogs. 3. Video
recordings—Catalogs. I. Title.
PN1995.9.W6A43 1999
016.79143'652042—DC21   99-25311

This book is printed on acid-free paper. (∞)

Printed in the United States of America
Designed by Miko McGinty

You can reach the author through her Web site at www.itgirlguide.com.

To Jess—

for indulging my fantasy by believing, and letting me believe,

that I am your glamorous leading lady.

Acknowledgments

Thanks to the following It Girls for their support and inspiration:
Miko McGinty, Rachel Tsutsumi, Toni Kohn, Sifu Sharon Wikel,
Ina Lewis, Jessica Swirnoff, Seanne Kemp-Kovach, Hallie Shano,
Michelle McElroy, Maria Kavanaugh, Diane Minter Lewis,
Carolyn Levy, Marla Levy, Jennifer Lytton, Carole "Bobo" Garven,
Julie Smooke, Carol Abrams, and Nora Gordon.
And special thanks to Jim at Beverly Hills Videocentre.

contents

introduction

Every girl can be an It Girl. She just needs to put a little effort into it. Don't worry—fun effort, not work effort. She throws fabulous parties, uses the word fabulous at every opportunity, sends flowers to a friend just because, carries the prettiest purse she can find— if even only to the market. To add some panache to her world she might need a little jump start. That's where these movies come in.

Just think, what would I be like if I were . . . say, Katharine Hepburn in *Bringing Up Baby*? A woman of leisure who dresses in black tie *every day*. A woman who is sure of what she wants and goes after it. A woman who knows she's quirky and makes no apologies. A woman who's confident without being cocky, who allows herself to just BE. Is this sounding like a Calvin Klein perfume ad? Not where I was going with it.

Isn't this the whole idea of movies? To put yourself in other people's shoes (which in this case would be beautiful alligator square-toe pumps). To imagine what things would be like if you were IN the story. Whether it's *Independence Day* or *A Room with a View*, the whole idea is to escape your life and get into someone else's. But we don't get to watch movies all day, so I recommend that you take pieces of these films with you. When I pop in one of these videos I get to live in a huge house with servants and a stable out back. I get to have men romance and dazzle me. And most important, let's not forget the effortless glamour with which I live my life (for those ninety minutes).

What was up with all that glamour? Where the hell can I get that? It seems to be a totally lost element today. I've given this a lot of thought so I might as well share my theory with you. Maybe the glamour was a product of the inequality between genders. Now, before you start calling me names, I'm not antifeminism. I love voting and stuff. But back then women were treated differently. Men would actually stand up when a woman entered the room (crazy, I know). And I think because of things like that women treated themselves differently. They seemed to always be on their best behavior in public, and they certainly took the time to put together a matchy-matchy outfit. In retrospect it gives us a view of a more *romantic* (albeit unequal) world. So now you know my secret. I'm simply a hopeless romantic. What? It's not a crime.

What's that? You're a closet romantic, too? Well, see, I knew we'd get along. You now have in your hot little hands a list of one hundred films. Though not all Oscar winners, these particular classics are all female driven. We enter the movie's world through the eyes of the manicured It Girl heroine. Remember: the fantasy element is heavy. Add that to the time warp and generation gap and we have a lot of unfamiliar territory to explore. All I really want is a little inspiration. Is that so wrong?

Here's my point: All girls want to feel beautiful. Right? Right. Inspiration is the road to achieving that very feeling. We all don't look like Cindy Crawford—generic example, I know—but we can achieve the feeling of being a super model if we get passionate about something. Anything. Once the video has been rewound ("be kind" and all that) and returned to the neighborhood rental joint, a piece of that It Girl is still there in you. I've been able to steal

Audrey Hepburn fixes her already perfect hair on the set of *Sabrina*, 1954.

morsels of inspiration from all of these movies. Whether it be an hour and a half of pure escapism (everyone could use that), a flirty wink, an air of confidence, or a delicious gown, I continue to add to my encyclopedia of passion fueling style and strength from these one hundred films. I hope you can, too.

And now for my disclaimer. I'm obviously very psyched about all of these movies: the romance, the corny manners, the beyond gorgeous clothes. The truth is that I wanted to write DON'T MISS or RENT THIS NOW under each title. I'm practically sitting on my hands

Grace Kelly fixes *her* already perfect hair on the set of *High Society*, 1956.

so as not to add this disruption. Just feel my pain and catch my drift on the excitement vibe. Also, please excuse that I surely have left out another one hundred or more great old films. I chose these for no other reason than I love watching them. Perhaps your favorite is missing—I had to stop somewhere (anyway, if it's your favorite, then you already know about it so don't get your nosejob out of joint).

You'll notice that some actresses were just too fabulous to list only once. Some of these leading ladies have so much to add in the inspiration department. Grace Kelly and Katharine Hepburn come to mind when I think of an It Girl for the ages. I also missed a couple of great actresses such as Dolores Del Rio and Gloria Swanson. So little room, so much attitude.

I know you're working on the career thing, and the relationship stuff is a lifetime upkeep, but don't forget to think about *you*! Go ahead, take some time away from that computer (or whatever monster you face daily). Let's be selfish. Fantasy is equal to oxygen—I'm not a scientist but just go with it. Watch a video, wear lipstick to the mailbox, take a bubble bath, pin your hair up. Let the glamour of a bygone decade live on. Feed your inner IT!

Sincerely, Clara Bow

It Girl

The expression It Girl comes from silver screen star Clara Bow. In 1927 she starred in a movie called *It*, and as you can imagine, because you're quick like that, she was referred to as the "It Girl." Sadly, ironically, and somehow blasphemously, none of her films are in this book. I know, it's morally wrong, but let's be honest—who really has time for silent movies?

the look

Whatever it is about these movies that carries me away (thanks, but no thanks, Calgon), it's mostly about the clothes. I know I'm shallow but at the very least, I'm honest. Somehow I equate a stunning outfit—matching hat, shoes, gloves, and bag—with a better life. You'd just have to have it all under control if you could pull off that look every day. Today, however, we can't go to the movies seeking style tips. You might get ideas from magazines or from the parade of gowns on Oscar night—modern actresses tend to dress better in life than in film. It's totally inconsistent with what it meant to be a star in the golden age of Hollywood. There was a total package. Back then they were always ready for the paparazzi and were dressed to the nines in every movie frame. My point being, have you ever seen a snapshot of Audrey Hepburn at an airport sporting Adidas sweatpants?

Audrey Hepburn with THE LOOK in *Breakfast at Tiffany's*, 1961.

Breakfast at Tiffany's

1961. Don't be discouraged by its popularity; it's still worth seeing at least three to five times. The poise with which Holly Golightly approaches her confused world is not only a great peek into 1961 New York City, but also a sideways glance at the heart of a little girl with too much style (I think we all know how painful that can be). But what does "fifty dollars for the powder room" mean anyway? See the perfect little black dress.

To Catch a Thief

1955. Grace Kelly AND Cary Grant! What more could you ask for? Oh, wait . . . it's on the French Riviera—forget about it! Fast cars, cool beach cabanas, a jewel thief, and a masquerade ball. Kelly plays a snoopy thrill-seeking heiress guarding her mother's jewels. As usual, Hitchcock keeps you guessing until the end.

A New Kind of Love

1963. If you're feeling ugly or unfeminine, you can always go to Paris and pose as a hooker to catch the eye of your man. That's what Joanne Woodward does in this Technicolor comedy about a newspaper sportswriter and a fashion designer. Paul Newman's just such a writer. These two married for real in 1958 and are still together today. Great Edith Head costumes, and a hidden identity mixes up the story line. Worth watching for those cute visuals (see the photo that talks back) and a radical fashion show.

Grace Kelly sets the bait in *To Catch a Thief*, 1955.

Designing Woman 1957. Not a new story—

newspaperman marries glamour girl. Gregory Peck (major stuffin')
is drunk at the Beverly Hills Hotel; meets Lauren Bacall; they fall
in love and marry, only to return to New York, where he finds she's
not who he thought she was. She's an uptown fashion designer
with a trust fund (he must be so disappointed). In this movie, Lauren
Bacall is everything I've ever wanted to be—beautiful *and* talented.
Admit you want to be her, too. Plotwise, be warned, the first half is
better than the second.

All About Eve 1950. Bette Davis is a theater diva who's

getting a little long in the tooth when an idolizing fan, played by
Anne Baxter, steps in. The premise seems to parallel the lives of
these actors. Gary Merrill is Davis's lover, whom she believes to be
trading her in for a younger model. George Sanders is the great
bitchy playwright. This film won six Oscars, including best picture
and costumes by Edith Head.

After the Thin Man 1936. I'm in LOVE with Myrna

Loy and William Powell. They're fabulous together. She wears great
attitude. Her suits and hats are fab. She's the rich, sophisticated girl
who marries a PI from the wrong side of the tracks. You get the
impression that they love being Nick and Nora Charles. Plus a very
chic fox terrier named Asta makes it all so thirties. There are five
Thin Man movies. This is number two. Why not rent them all and
have your own film festival?

Edith Head

Edith Head made a living making other women look amazing. In 1924, she "borrowed" the artwork of fellow students and passed it off as her own, landing the job of sketch artist at Paramount. She worked her way up to costume designer, where she stayed for 44 years. She then moved over to Universal and stayed until 1981, the year she died. Working on 750 films, she had 35 Oscar nominations and walked away with 8 of them. She rocked the fashion world. She also made *Vogue* patterns and did a stint on *The Art Linkletter Show* called "Advice to the Unchic." We need to see reruns pronto!

There were other great costume designers from these films: Irene, Jean Louis, and Adrian to name a few. I just remember noticing Edith's name on all my favorites since birth.

marriage

I, myself, am just a beginner. I've been at the
marriage thing only a year or so, and I'm not about
to go spewing advice . . . for once. I actually do love
it, and having your best friend around 24/7 is a
slice of heaven. The funny thing about these movies
is that they all have married couples who obviously
are meant to be together forever, and in each case
they're trying to get a *divorce*! I didn't plan it that way;
these are just the movies I love. GO FIG! I guess the
simple idea of spending the rest of your days with
one person is cause for conflict and comedy.

I know I wasn't going to ooh and aah and tell you
how much I love a flick, but *The Awful Truth* is just
so great I'm demanding you see it for your own
well-being. If you don't, well, let's just say I won't
be held responsible for my actions.

Joel McCrea can't keep his pants on around Claudette Colbert in *The Palm
Beach Story*, 1942.

The Palm Beach Story 1942. My favorite

Preston Sturges romantic comedy. It's a silly story that (like most of
these) is hard to relate to. Claudette Colbert, loving her husband and
thinking herself a financial drain with her expensive lifestyle (*that*, I can
relate to), tries to divorce him and marry up in order to help support
him. She's all about alimony in reverse. Rudy Vallee is the nerdy
billionaire (no, duh), while Joel McCrea is the sweet loyal husband
who tries to stop her. A really fun way to spend an hour or so.

Two for the Road 1967. An amazing inside look

at the life span of a marriage. Albert Finney and Audrey Hepburn
meet while traveling through Europe as young adults. Their lives
together—for better *and* for worse—are chronicled through the trips
they take. On the bumpy road of life their union is one big pothole.
This film shows moments in a marriage that no one ever sees.
It's the awkwardness of being a fly on the wall with the pleasure
of getting to ride through the countryside.

Mr. & Mrs. Smith 1941. Robert Montgomery and

Carole Lombard are happily wed, most of the time, when they
discover their marriage license is nonbinding. A great screwball
comedy directed by Alfred Hitchcock (the murders must be on
the cutting-room floor). There's a scene in this movie that kills me
every time I see it, and there aren't many laugh-out-loud-really-
hard-even-when-you're-alone times in most of these videos.

Bedtime for Bouffant. Albert Finney and Audrey Hepburn in *Two for the
Road*, 1967.

The Awful Truth 1937. Believe me when I tell you that
this is, in fact, my favorite movie. Irene Dunne and Cary Grant are
married, in love, and trying to get a divorce. Of course, it's all due
to one misunderstanding after another. Mr. Smith is their wonderful
terrier, and Ralph Bellamy plays the rich Texan who's after Dunne.
The rapport between Dunne and Grant is the absolute best of the
witty dialogue from the thirties. Her hat in the courtroom scene not
only defies gravity but all laws of accessories as well. DO NOT MISS
THIS ONE!

The Perfect Marriage 1946. On their tenth
anniversary, David Niven and Loretta Young decide to call it quits.
Luckily, their respective parents, who hate each other, become the
meddling in-laws who just may save the day. Niven and Young's
darling daughter, Cookie, and all of their gossipy friends add to the
mix. You do get a bit tense observing their hostilities, and I found
that after watching it, I couldn't shake the tension. Convincing
acting or PMS, you be the judge.

The Grass Is Greener 1961. Deborah Kerr and
Cary Grant are proper, English, and live in a swank palace. When
American tourist Robert Mitchum (looking like a droopy dog—
he's no match for Grant) takes the palace tour, he stumbles into a
private room where he immediately falls in love with Kerr. Grant
confides in his wife's friend, Jean Simmons. Watch as these four
discuss matters of the heart like a hand of bridge. Totally charming
and ultracivilized. Visual bonus points for Jean's wardrobe!

Irene Dunne feeds Cary Grant's terrier in *The Awful Truth*, 1937.

Lauren Bacall eyes her on-screen hubby, Fred MacMurray, in *Woman's World*, 1954.

being a wife

This seems to be the MO for most women before the invention of your VCR. In the days of wine and roses, a wife was mainly just that. It was what you did all day long: took care of the house, raised children, made yourself look pretty with a weekly hairdo, and had a hot meal on the table at 6:00 P.M.* Anyway, even with the new millennium upon us, a lot of the same principles apply. *Love* and *honor*. But I am pretty sure they took out the *obey* part. Some bleeding heart probably got uppity and made a stink.

* Pssst—insider's info—at my house the just-add-water kind of noodle soup is served at 8:30 P.M., and my hair is in a perpetual ponytail. And don't you feel that you and I are just that much closer since I've opened up with a glimpse of my über-glamorous life?

Linda Darnell, Ann Sothern, and Jeanne Crain with the mail in *A Letter to Three Wives*, 1949.

Woman's World 1954. Before divorce was the standard, standing behind your man was a pretty serious job for most wives . . . so I've learned. Three top executives of a national company are being considered to succeed the president. All of the nominees and their wives come together for the final exam at the New York headquarters, where the prez has cooked up a scheme to pick the best man based on his wife. June Allyson, Lauren Bacall, and Arlene Dahl. This one's a keeper!

A Letter to Three Wives 1949. The title *is* the story. Addie Ross is the woman we never see although she narrates the entire film. Three different couples, all close friends, share Addie Ross. She is adored by the husbands and hated by the wives, played by Jeanne Crain, Linda Darnell, and Ann Sothern. When the four girls plan an outing, Addie sends a letter in her absence. The letter explains that she's run off with one of their husbands. Which one?

Barefoot in the Park 1967. Jane Fonda is determined to make a home out of a decrepit old studio apartment for her and new husband/lawyer, Robert Redford. This Neil Simon play turned movie is really about the struggle of being wifely in the late sixties. Do you do what your mother did? And what *did* your mother do? It does feel very theatery as almost every scene takes place in the one-room studio.

The Bishop's Wife 1947. Cary Grant is an angel
(tell me something I don't know). In this Christmas story, he comes
down from heaven to answer the prayers of preacher David Niven.
Niven's church is in dire straits and his wife, Loretta Young, is
slipping away. Grant and Young develop a special friendship. I can't
wait to get to heaven if Grant is any indication of what angels are
like. Also colorized—pass!

Who's Got the Action? 1962. Dean Martin
plays the gambling-crazed husband to Lana Turner. Totally fed up,
she pretends to be his silent bookie in order to save their home.
She collects the bets just when his luck turns. Between Eddie
Albert's advances and having to sell off her antiques to pay her
husband, she's pretty cool, not to mention resourceful. Walter
Matthau has a terrific cameo. Dazzling Technicolor.

technicolor

This term you'll see often and even though I use it as a
description, I don't know what I'm talking about. When I'm
watching a movie that's bright and the colors are groovy, I
just think it's "Technicolor." But the reality is that this is the
trade name for a specific kind of color processing. Without
getting too science nerd . . . it was used like lithography
offset printing. They worked from three-color dyes. The
colors were added, one at a time, to a clear film to make it
look this way—like eye candy. One tidbit worth mentioning
is its aftermath. Because this process needed a lot of light,
seriously high wattage was dumped on those sets and
some actresses in later years developed a codependency
on their sunglasses.

letterbox

If you have a choice between letterbox or not, go for box.
When you're at home watching, you'll feel like you get to see
less of the screen, but in those tricky and technical ways,
you actually get to see more. When they (you know, *they*)
format film to television, they chop off the sides to make it
fit. In letterbox format, you get to see the original the way it
appeared in the theaters (without the squeaky chairs).

Mom's bad timing. Ann Blyth and Zachary Scott are interrupted by Joan Crawford in *Mildred Pierce*, 1945.

motherhood

Being a mother is a lifetime job; however, the part that is so often the attention getter is the pregnancy. You get fat, sick, tired, sometimes you even look your best—whatever. The weird part is that in the olden days girls never revealed a big ol' tummy the way we do now. There was something taboo about it. I even read that the famous purse, the Hermès Kelly bag, was named because Princess Grace used it to cover her pregnant belly in public. How funny is that compared to that awesome photo of a totally nude Demi Moore with child on *Vanity Fair*'s cover? I bring this up because none of the motherhood pics show or talk about the P word (NO! Not penis—get your mind out of the gutter for once). Being an It Girl means that one day, if you're not already, most likely you'll be a mom or at the very least a terrific doting aunt. Watch these.

Mildred Pierce 1945. Joan Crawford is a single

mother who only wants to make enough money to support her daughters. Working as a waitress, she learns the restaurant business and eventually cleans up. Meanwhile, her brat of a daughter who's embarrassed by her mother proves it by making a play for mom's man. Crawford got the Oscar. Ann Blyth is a great little bitch. I used to think this film was too dramatic to hold my interest, if that makes sense, but after seeing it again recently, I stand corrected. As usual.

Auntie Mame 1958. Everyone wishes they had

an Auntie Mame or maybe wishes that they *were* Auntie Mame. Rosalind Russell is the eccentric wealthy actress writing her memoirs between cocktail parties when her nephew, Patrick, comes to live with her. In raising the boy from elementary school age to engagement, Mame *makes* this family and lends her generous spirit to everything she does. She's over the top, loud, super glam, and loving to a fault.

The Lady Is Willing 1942. Marlene Dietrich and

Fred MacMurray—an unlikely pair in the first place. He's a child-hating pediatrician (you heard me) just trying to do his research. She's a Broadway star in love with an orphaned infant she's fighting to keep. I not only love the clothes, the apartment, and the romance, but also the wisecracking assistant played by Aline MacMahon.

Rosalind Russell is everyone's favorite untamed relative in *Auntie Mame*, 1958.

In Name Only 1939. Carole Lombard is a widow
who just wants a quiet life for herself and her daughter in the
country. Along comes Cary Grant, the charming neighbor (wanna
borrow a cup of sugar? wink, nudge). He's trapped in a marriage
of convenience to fabulously wicked Kay Francis. Some very
tragic twists occur, and don't be surprised if you shed a tear or
two for Lombard.

Please Don't Eat the Daisies 1960. The
odd coupling of super British David Niven to all-American Doris Day
is a great start. He's a New York theater critic and she's a suburban
housewife/mom. This film covers a short span of time in the dreamy
lives of these people. I wouldn't mind watching more of their life as
it unfolds. Be warned, you may want to turn down the volume when
the theme song starts up. It's one of those infectious tunes you
could be humming for days. Let's not forget the BIG selling point,
their amazingly cute sheep dog.

Cary Grant

"Everybody wants to be Cary Grant, even Cary Grant." This having been said by the man himself just about proves my point. Born Archibald Leach in England in 1904, he began his theatrical career early as a mime (now say how much you hate mimes) and went on to star in seventy-two films. Having once met Douglas Fairbanks, he modeled himself after the perfect gentleman, breaking hearts steadily throughout his career. Audrey Hepburn in *Charade* said, "You know what's wrong with you? Nothing."

sibling stories

I've personally always been obsessed with wanting a sister. Someone you can love and abuse, and she'll always be there? *Three Smart Girls* is just the kind of heavy-duty sister-bonding movie that we sisterless women crave (even if these girls are a bit weird since they're super rich and yet they all sleep in one room). A couple of these flicks dive headlong into the sticky issue of sibling rivalry—the grass is always greener. . . . Anyway, the family dynamic is just too complicated not to have its own chapter. But don't be scared off—there's no *Ordinary People* deep subject matter here, just lighthearted laughs throughout all of these pics.

An Audrey Hepburn sandwich for Humphrey Bogart and William Holden in a publicity still for *Sabrina*, 1954.

Cheers to a mahvalous pahty, dahling! Jean Dixon, Cary Grant, Katharine Hepburn, and Lew Ayres raise their glasses in *Holiday*, 1938.

Sabrina 1954. When your father's a chauffeur and you live above the garage, you get a great view of the playground of the rich and handsome. Audrey Hepburn is Sabrina, who's in love with one of the Larrabee brothers, William Holden (man, he's cute). She's sent to cooking school in Paris, where she learns to be a real lady. Upon her return home, she begins to see the attributes of the *other* Larrabee brother, a no-nonsense Humphrey Bogart. Another great Audrey-gets-a-haircut movie (see *Roman Holiday*) and the winner of the most-creative-place-to-hide-champagne-flutes award.

Holiday 1938. A bittersweet romance with *some* comedy but not a romantic comedy. Cary Grant is Johnny Case, who's about to marry into a wealthy Fifth Avenue family. After meeting his sister-in-law-to-be, Katharine Hepburn, things take a turn. Her struggle with herself and her environment makes you want to reach out and hug her, especially because she looks so comfortable in formal attire. She's the black sheep of the family, and he's a young banker on the rise looking for more than money. Check out Grant and Hepburn's matching side parts that make them look extra young.

Three Smart Girls 1936. If you don't mind a

little singing (feel free to hit that FF button), then this is the sister movie for you. Deanna Durbin (Universal's answer to MGM's Judy Garland) and her two screen sisters travel from Switzerland to New York. They need to break up the upcoming marriage of their father to a society gold digger. A very sweet romance blooms where least expected. Charles Winninger is the absentminded, stuttering, skirt-chasing dad. Really cute family movie.

My Man Godfrey 1957. Get this June Allyson

remake of the equally great original 1936 movie. Two sisters try to beat each other in the family scavenger hunt. June wins when she brings home a hobo (David Niven) whom she then puts to work as the house butler. Little does she know he's not really a hobo (nice word by the way). June is the ultimate girl next door in this you-could-never-have-a-plot-like-this-today movie (and we're not counting *Down and Out in Beverly Hills*) so enjoy it!

fat dads

My dad? Not fat. Most old movie dads? Total blubber. I don't
have any explanation for this, except maybe that it makes
them look more endearing or something. Check out *Three
Smart Girls*, *I Married a Witch*, *It Happened One Night*, and
the list goes on.

dahling

A term of endearment I think we need to work together to
bring back into style. Begin to incorporate it in your daily
vocab. A tip: Go for more Holly Golightly and less Zsa Zsa.
Need help using it in a sentence? "Dahling, would you mind,
terribly, removing the pickle from my Big Mac?" No time like
the present to start.

magic

Be honest, you adored *Bewitched* and *I Dream of Jeannie*. You wanted to have magical powers, and you even loved the movie *Escape to Witch Mountain*. This stuff falls under the indulge-your-fantasy category (also see the princess complex in the ROYALTY chapter). It always seems to be us chicks who are into the voodoo. Could it be the female spiritual connection to things otherworldly: witches, ghosts, pixies, fairies? Mother Nature (huh?). Buffy the Vampire Slayer? I don't have the answers. Let's face it, I barely have the questions. All I know is that my nose is still screwed up from trying to make it twitch.

Fredric March under the spell of Veronica Lake in *I Married a Witch*, 1942.

I Married a Witch

1942. After being burned at the stake, Veronica Lake (doesn't she ever want to pull that hair back into a ponytail?) is a witch who's back in the land of the living. Too bad everyone she knew is already dead. Her plan of revenge will have to be played out on the descendants of her murderer. Lake's too busy trying to have a good time, so her also dead warlock dad ends up doing the dirty work, which, you can imagine, is very dirty considering they're witches.

Portrait of Jennie

1948. A haunting love story about a starving artist, Joseph Cotten, and his muse. Jennifer Jones plays girl-turned-woman as they magically cross some twilight-zone time warp. She asks him to wait for her to grow up and, lucky for him, it only takes about half an hour. Today it could have some weird pedophilic angle especially because he picks her up in the park. His painting finally comes to life (not literally) when he does her portrait.

Blithe Spirit

1945. Poor Rex Harrison. Little did he know that a casual séance would bring back the spirit of his first wife. This might not be so horrible except that it's quite an inconvenience for his present wife. A *great plot* plays out when wife number one tries to kill Rex so they can be together again. Constance Cummings and Kay Hammond are the wives—two British birds I'd not known. And don't miss the wacky bike-riding madam.

Joseph Cotten eats the earlobe of his muse, Jennifer Jones, in *Portrait of Jennie*, 1948.

Topper 1937. A romantic-comedy ghost story. Constance Bennett (so suave) and Cary Grant (terminally suave) are the wealthy, carefree, and glamorous Kirbys who die in a car accident and must complete a good deed in order to get to heaven. They decide to haunt Mr. Topper, their bank president, and show him how to loosen his tie. The first half is better than the second, and the special effects aren't bad for 1937. Hedda Hopper has a cameo as socialite Mrs. Stuyvesant.

Supernatural 1933. Carole Lombard, Randolph Scott (cute love interest), and Alan Dinehart (super bad guy). OK, try to stay with me on this one. This is a *crazy* story about the reincarnated spirit of a murderess who takes over the body of Lombard. Lombard is in the midst of mourning the loss of her twin brother. The psychic who claims to bring back the twin just so happens to be the murderess's murderer! Got it? Good. Get it.

Bell, Book and Candle 1958. If you like the magic stuff, add this one for sure. Kim Novak and her cat, Piewackit, charm Jimmy Stewart. Getting involved with a witch is hard enough, but when you throw in Jack Lemmon as her warlock brother, the plot thickens. She's way sexy but her ash blond hair has gotta go (yuck).

Bette Davis models the latest chapeau in this publicity still from the early 1930s.

hats

I'm lucky to be one of the few who can actually wear hats. I'm not bragging; it's just a fact. But that's not my point. The point is that in a simpler, more civilized time, women wore matching hats with practically EVERY ensemble. Sadly, living in sunny, funny LA, I have to wait for bad weather to visit the milliner. If you're a millinophile like me, don't miss *The Millionairess*.

pure romance

Most, if not all, of the movies in this guidebook have
at least a morsel of romance, as all movies ever
made should (I'm trying to pass a law). I thought at
some point we should just cut the crap and get to
the goods. We can really focus our I-need-to-find-a-
good-love-story energy here. Are we in it for any
other reason? I know not. So here's the stuff we're
looking for, and whether or not we've found it in
real life, this is the backup plan: heavily buttered
popcorn, large diet Coke, and all of the films in this
chapter.* Also note the Judy Holliday film. I was really
resistant to being in her fan club, but I've since
broken down and joined. (OK, not literally—I'm not
that much of a nerd. I think.)

*Another nugget of advice: if you spill a bag of M&Ms directly
into the bowl of popcorn, you not only save time, but you get
the simultaneous sugar rush with the grease, salt, and crunch
of the corn.

Gary Cooper is new to giving pedicures as Barbara Stanwyck awaits hers
in *Ball of Fire*, 1941.

Ball of Fire 1941. Barbara Stanwyck is the tough

mobster's moll. On the run from the law and the mob (they want
her to marry the boss so she can't testify against him), she finds
sanctuary in the middle of seven men writing an encyclopedia (that
happens to me all the time). The bookish Gary Cooper falls hard
in this modern (although now old) Snow White. Cute opposites-
attract vibe and amusing background with dwarfish academi-acs.

Nothing Sacred 1937. Another favorite. Carole

Lombard is a small-town girl diagnosed with radiation poisoning
(ouch). Fredric March is a newspaperman in desperate need of
a story. He brings her to New York City in her dying days. She
becomes the mascot, inspiration, and toast of the town. *Then* the
movie starts and the twists begin. I love this one and, as usual,
Carole's awesome. Look for a Hedda Hopper cameo.

How to Steal a Million 1966. I wasn't a Peter

O'Toole fan until I saw this one (but try to see *Lawrence of Arabia*
on the big screen if you ever get the chance). Audrey Hepburn
must steal her family's loaned statue from the museum before it's
discovered a fake. O'Toole is her burglar for hire, and Eli Wallach
wants her for his bride. Great physical comedy from O'Toole hiding
in a broom closet. Audrey's mod styling proves that any clothes *too*
hip really look silly in retrospect. Eli gives Audrey a ring that would
make any girl drool buckets.

Fredric March plays hard to get with Carole Lombard in *Nothing Sacred*, 1937.

Born Yesterday

1950. Judy Holliday (with her trying voice) won an Oscar for this performance. She's the ditzy girlfriend of wealthy low-class Broderick Crawford. Embarrassed by her in his political circles, Crawford hires William Holden to be her tutor. Much to Crawford's chagrin, she smartens up and enjoys it. I won't say any more except that romance *does* blossom with her newfound intellect.

Dream Wife

1953. Cary Grant and Deborah Kerr together again (catch *The Grass Is Greener* and *An Affair to Remember*). This time they work for the government, and it's Kerr's job to teach Grant the protocol of marrying an Eastern princess. (No, not the Upper East Side.) Available in either black and white or color. Although I wouldn't normally encourage it, go for color; get crazy, you only live once, and besides, it makes the Eastern garb and decor look great.

Midnight

1939. Down-on-her-luck singer Claudette Colbert is about to lose her cool and fall in love with a very cute and very poor cab driver, Don Ameche. Fleeing from him and her fear of commitment, she hides in the world of the rich and famous. Acting as a fake countess, she does a bit of marriage counseling. It's even more complicated than it sounds. This sweet Cinderella story has amusing characters from the upper-crust set. Yet another smashing Hedda Hopper cameo.

Judy Holliday on the rise in *Born Yesterday*, 1950.

Anthony Dawson wants to accessorize Grace Kelly's outfit in *Dial M for Murder*, 1954.

scary

I'm *so* not the scary movie kind of girl. I hate jump-out-and-scare-you, bludgeon-you-to-death-with-a-large-dull-object, stab-you, rape-you, drive-over-your-car-and-smush-you stuff (although I am rather fond of the word "bludgeon"). I embarrassingly had a week's worth of nightmares from *Fargo*. Something about that wood chipper was making me uneasy. That said, these movies are all SUSPENSE-driven scary, and that in and of itself is enough for me. This chapter might be a bit pedestrian for those of you who are fans of *Scream*. Sorry, but I can only take so much fear in one lifetime, and cardiac arrest isn't my favorite way to spend a night at the movies. HEY! I heard that! Don't call me a baby! I'm not a baby! I CAN watch those movies; maybe I just don't WANT to.

A few notes: A) Three out of four of these films are by Hitchcock—coincidence. B) Three out of four of these films involve husband wanting wife dead—scary. C) Three out of four dentists surveyed recommend—just kidding.

Dial M for Murder 1954. Grace Kelly is perfect—

no wonder she became a princess. Her clothes are simple and chic
while looking very expensive. She's a victim of her husband's greed
and brilliance in a love-triangle plot that's complex without being too
hard to follow. Ray Milland is evil and British at the same time in this
originally 3-D movie.

Shadow of a Doubt 1943. Joseph (black hat)

Cotten is the favorite uncle to his namesake niece, Charley (Teresa
Wright). With his odd and nervous behavior, she suspects he may
be the wife killer described in the newspapers. Great secondary
characters. Watch for the banter between father and neighbor as
they parallel the story by trying for fun to plot the perfect murder.
Take note: this one *is* scary (for me anyway, which means not at
all to most people. Kinda like spicy food. Sometimes toothpaste is
too spicy for me, but I digress).

Suspicion 1941. Cary Grant is a dapper, sought-after

bachelor (hard to imagine), so who would've guessed that he'd
want to marry Joan Fontaine, the well-bred spinster? As they begin
their lives together, Joan suspects he's out to kill her for her money.
Is he? Joan won the Oscar for Best Actress. Well deserved. See
for yourself.

Gaslight

1944. Serious Ingrid Bergman. Sadly for her, she's in a loveless marriage and to make matters worse, her husband is doing his best to drive her insane (I know we've all felt that way with a husband or boyfriend at *least* once). Thank God for Joseph (white hat) Cotten, who steps in to try to help. A spooky story (not by Hitchcock, believe it or not). Bergman won an Oscar. A definite rainy-day pick; in fact, why not make it a double feature with *Anastasia*— on second thought, don't. Too much drama might result in a nap.

Charles Boyer tightens his grip on Ingrid Bergman in *Gaslight*, 1944.

beauty

Remember how I mentioned that these Hollywood women always had the outfit thing down? Well, it's the same with hair and makeup. Of course. How come I can spend two hours with the hair dryer and still have to face the world with a bad-hair day? Just lucky, I guess. I think the rules were different then, and you pretty much couldn't show up in public in a baseball cap and tennis shoes unless, of course, you were playing baseball or tennis. Grooming seems to be a pretty high priority for these women of the "olden days." Let's check out what a little makeup and lighting can do for a girl (or guy, as the case may be).

Make sure you notice the getup on Rosalind Russell just for an afternoon visit with her friend Joan Crawford. And what's with Joan in that bubble bath in the middle of the day? See what I mean about the importance of grooming?

Rosalind Russell, looking otherworldly, thinks Joan Crawford is all washed up in *The Women*, 1939.

The Women

1939. A favorite of gay men worldwide. It shows women of the thirties with more sass than RuPaul. They ask for Jungle Red at the manicurist, which is the code for "gimme the gossip." The cast is made up entirely of women. It's catty, funny, and has an amazing wardrobe. Norma Shearer, Rosalind Russell, and Joan Crawford rock! Hedda Hopper has a cameo.(And don't miss the 1956 musical version, *The Opposite Sex*.)

Some Like It Hot

1959. The original *Tootsie*. These musical "girls" are hiding out from the mob in a troupe of traveling gold diggers. Cute story and amusing cross-dressing moments as both Jack Lemmon and Tony Curtis fall for Marilyn, who looks fabulous in a quirky sexy kind of way. Do you think that no one really suspected they were men? Hard to say.

Jack Lemmon awaits his make-under in *Some Like It Hot*, 1959.

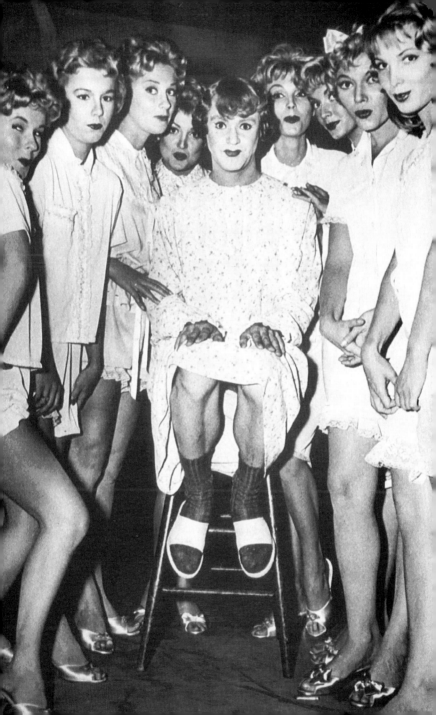

Beauty for the Asking 1939. Finally, a Lucille

Ball vehicle! Although she isn't doing the slapstick she's now
famous for, she's so likable as the ambitious aesthetician
(translation: "beautician"). Lucy invents a cure-all face cream.
Looking for investors, like the new woman of her old, old man,
Lucy finds a way to make everything work to her advantage.

Will Success Spoil Rock Hunter?

1957. Not totally female driven, although the movie does revolve
around lipstick. Great opening sequence. Tony Randall is a
writer at an advertising firm, and Betsy Drake is his wholesome
girlfriend/secretary. Randall hires Jayne Mansfield, the bombshell,
as the spokeswoman for his lipstick campaign. Don't miss
Mansfield's matching poodle with each ensemble. Joan Blondell
is the wonderful assistant to Mansfield and refers to herself as
"the writer's subplot."

The diva studies her dialogue. Bette Davis on the set of *Now, Voyager*, 1942.

cigarettes

More than 400,000 Americans die annually due to smoking-related diseases. I'm not the first to tell you that smoking causes all kinds of nasty fatal illnesses, but I may be the first to tell you that in these movies, it just looks so damn glam! Whatever, it's all just part of the fantasy.

kooky capers

There's barely a hairline difference between screwball comedies, which began in the thirties, and just plain romantic comedies. You know, the "kooky" (great overused word) girl and the normal nice guy who gets caught up in her wild caper (another great word). These films are also known for some wonderful fast-paced witty repartee. I've spread the love and sprinkled screwballs throughout most of the book. These are just some classics to whet your appetite. (Note, however, that in *My Favorite Wife*, Cary Grant seems to be in the mixed-up "kooky" female role. Either way, it's still *screwy* and worth seeing.)

Clark Gable and Claudette Colbert try an old-fashioned mode of transport in *It Happened One Night*, 1934.

It Happened One Night 1934. The first
Roman Holiday. Runaway heiress Claudette Colbert is discovered
and cared for by newspaper hound, Clark Gable. During a very
busy bus trip from Miami to New York, they fall for each other. They
arrive just in time for her wedding to someone else (surprised?), and
the third act doesn't let up. One of the very first screwball comedies.
Frank Capra walked away with all five major Oscars that year.

Bringing Up Baby 1938. Katharine Hepburn's acting
is always so effortless that she glides into this role as the kooky rich
girl with a pet leopard (Baby) without missing a beat. Cary Grant is
an endearing, albeit nerdy, paleontologist in search of a bone—pun
optional. A total film-class must see. Dumb story, but a beyond-cute
execution. And of course, Hepburn's tenacity enables her to get her
man. Point for the ladies.

My Favorite Wife 1940. The second of two Irene
Dunne and Cary Grant films I've listed (the first was my all-time
favorite, *The Awful Truth*). Dunne is the shipwrecked wife who finally
returns to her husband, Grant, and children. Her arrival coincides
with his honeymoon to the new wife, Gail Patrick. Dunne is fun
loving and witty while Patrick is straitlaced and snooty. Things get
even more complicated when Dunne's deserted-island companion
shows up. It's like some wacky double date gone wrong—we've
all been there.

Katharine Hepburn and Cary Grant leopard sit in *Bringing Up Baby*, 1938.

Director Ernst Lubitsch looks on while Gary Cooper and Claudette Colbert work things out in *Bluebeard's Eighth Wife*, 1938.

Bluebeard's Eighth Wife 1938. This would've

been in the GOLD DIGGER chapter, but I couldn't make one because it would end up including almost every movie in this book. Claudette Colbert meets him, she hates him, she loves him, she hates him, she loves him, she hates him, she loves him, he loves her . . . but wait, he hates her, he loves her. For my money, I usually prefer Joel McCrea to Gary Cooper as the straight guy, but this one works.

Two-Faced Woman 1941. Greta Garbo meets

Melvyn Douglas. The plot is an episode of *I Love Lucy* but is fun in its own way. It's a familiar-feeling story of a woman pretending to be her own twin sister to get the attention of her husband. He, of course, knows all along. The best part of this film, besides Garbo's thick Swedish accent, is the cute, cute, *cute* Ruth Gordon as Douglas's secretary and Garbo's confidante. The movie is all the sweeter when you know it was Garbo's swan song.

The Lady Eve 1941. A Preston Sturges film. LOVE.

Barbara Stanwyck is a cruise-ship con artist. Her shtick as the tough guy is pretty good. Cute opening credits. Again a woman in love pretends to be her own twin to get her man. This time it's Henry Fonda, who, by the way, is really appealing.

get the kleenex

This is the only truly intense part of our book. I mean, it's not *Schindler's List* in Technicolor, but these movies are thought provoking (I know, I should've kept it all light, but . . .). They're also heartbreaking and infuriating. When you're in no mood for Doris Day, this is the section for you. If you're looking for a good cry (and who isn't?) or if you just need to be alone brooding, these are the ones to watch. Sometimes what will happen is that a sad story bigger than your own (if you have one) will put everything into perspective, and then you'll end up feeling great about your life. Or maybe it will be nothing more than a ninety-minute escape, and I should shut up. Either way, keep this list handy for rainy days (I'll also allow overcast) when all you can do is curl up on the couch with blanky and pilly. And turn out the lights for added ambiance; just please don't fall asleep. I don't pass all this wisdom on to you for my health, you know.

Warren Beatty teaches Vivien Leigh the horizontal mambo in *The Roman Spring of Mrs. Stone*, 1961.

The Roman Spring of Mrs. Stone

1961. This is originally a Tennessee Williams novel. Vivien Leigh (Scarlet herself) is an aged theater actress who moves to Rome after the death of her older, wealthy husband. Apparently, there are a few of these widows looking for love. Luckily a ring of young gigolos helps these ladies forget their wrinkles and their loneliness (supply and demand). Warren Beatty is just such a gigolo. *Buon giorno* drama.

Dark Victory 1939. Bette Davis is a society girl with a brain tumor (bummer). Fortunately, to ease the pain, her doctor, George Brent, is in love with her. The finale brings me to buckets of tears every time I see it. Although I do have to laugh when Davis discovers her illness on her way to lunch and orders "Prognosis Negative!"

An Affair to Remember 1957. At first I didn't really get the connection between Deborah Kerr and Cary Grant, but as the film played out, I couldn't imagine how they'd ever be apart. Two people meet crossing the Atlantic on a luxury liner. They're engaged to other people so they have to lie low. They decide to meet in six months at the top of the Empire State Building. Try not to see the original *Love Affair* or the remake before you watch this. At least one box of tissues is required. Oh, man, this is such a good one!

The Children's Hour

1961. By far the heaviest of subject matter in our little book. By today's standards, it's nothing more than a sad story of ignorance feeding homophobia. By the standards of 1961, it was an incredibly risqué tale of two women whose lives are destroyed when they're accused of lesbianism. An infuriating film wonderfully directed by William Wyler. It stars Audrey Hepburn and Shirley MacLaine like you've never seen them before. Really.

Audrey Hepburn and Shirley MacLaine stand up for their rights in *The Children's Hour*, 1961.

Now, Voyager 1942. Bette Davis is the family spinster

who, for a small moment in time, blossoms to find love. Returning
from said voyage back to reality, she's condemned to living with her
mean old mother and sweet memories. Things begin to change
when she befriends the offspring of her sweetheart. Bittersweet.
Davis is amazing at being creepy yet sad.

Casablanca 1942. Not much to say; this one speaks

for itself. Bogart and Bergman are old lovers who meet again during
World War II. Bogart's aloof Rick isn't easy to read, but we all know
what he really means when he says, "Here's looking at you, kid."
I know you've seen it but just treat yourself again and get lost in
the passion.

The Apartment 1960. Best Picture, Best Director

(Billy Wilder, a name you should know), and Best Screenplay.
Although I expected to see both comedy and drama, I found it to
be mostly drama. Shirley MacLaine is incredible as the elevator
operator/boss's girlfriend. Jack Lemmon is the low-level exec who
kisses ass by letting the bigger execs use his pad for makin'
whoopee. I'm not getting into too much story—just rent it.

Bette Davis travels with her broken heart in *Now, Voyager*, 1942.

wisecracking second girl

Maybe it's because I was never the homecoming queen, or maybe I just love a good one-liner, but my favorite aspect in some of these films is the smart-ass assistant/friend. She's usually not as glamorous as the leading lady, but she's way more fun to be around.

the misunderstanding

I know that *Three's Company* did a great job of making every episode about a misunderstanding. This seems to be the basis for all light comedy. Sometimes it gets a bit annoying for the watcher but just go with it—it *moves* the story.

newspapermen

If I describe a leading man as having the job of a newspaperman more than a dozen times, just know it's not a typo. For
some reason or another, this seemed to be a popular
profession for a character. I guess it's better than the post
office.

Gregory Peck is on assignment with Audrey Hepburn in *Roman Holiday*, 1953.

getting the guy

Maybe I was absent that day, but I never really learned how or when to "work it." You know, the seduction thing, and make him think it's all his idea? There's the eyelash batting, the fallen hankie, and the raising of the hemline. Seriously, how corny can you get? Guess I'm just the down-to-earth, girl-next-door type. Here are six juicy videos where our heroines (not as in mainline) set out to land their men and actually DO it in most cases. There's an even mix of light to heavy, and I won't give it away, except to say that the heavy ones start with W. They range from harmlessly pathetic to outright claw scratchers. If you're looking for pointers, I think I'd stick to *Cosmopolitan* magazine, since these films are pretty outdated. On second thought, *Cosmo* never helped either. Sorry.

Debbie Reynolds plays it coy (NOT) with Frank Sinatra in *The Tender Trap*, 1955.

The Tender Trap 1955. Although they sing the title

song of this movie one or two too many times, Debbie Reynolds is as cute as a button trying to win over the ultimate bachelor in Frank Sinatra. It's that simple with a few complexities of the heart and his large "little black book." Nice to see ol' blue eyes sweat out his Casanova persona.

How to Marry a Millionaire 1953. How

politically incorrect can you get? Three women set themselves up in a fancy apartment to land any available big-city men. Their scheme involves selling off the furniture in order to buy nice clothes (OK, that wasn't such a crazy idea). Lauren Bacall is the super cool leader. Marilyn Monroe, in my favorite of her roles, is the nearsighted four eyes. Betty Grable plays the boring, middle-of-the-road one. They find their men, only (ooh, I feel a twist coming on) you can't guess who they end up being.

Every Girl Should Be Married 1948.

Betsy Drake is pathetic as she makes a full-time job out of trying to land the handsome pediatrician, Cary Grant. Maybe it wasn't so pathetic after all, because they married in real life at about the same time. There's a twist at the end followed by another twist just for good measure.

All eight eyes of Marilyn Monroe and David Wayne watch Lauren Bacall in
How to Marry a Millionaire, 1953.

The World of Suzie Wong 1960. A tragic

love story (don't worry, happy ending). Nancy Kwan is a Chinese
call girl who likes to live in a fantasy world to avoid her sad life.
William Holden is an architect turned painter who comes to Hong
Kong. They meet and she becomes his muse before he becomes
her love. A sort of *Pretty Woman* vibe, and this is Nancy's first film.

That Touch of Mink 1962. Doris Day is a hard-

working single girl who gets a splash of wealthy bachelor Cary
Grant. Wanting him, she does what all women think about doing:
she makes an elaborate plan to manipulate him into wanting her.
Using his best friend, Gig Young (so likable), and the slimy Beasley,
played by John Astin, she sets the bait. Don't be shocked when I
tell you that it's a Doris Day kind of movie—what did you expect?—
and it really hits the spot when you're in the mood for an upbeat
and silly romance.

When Ladies Meet 1941. Guy loves girl who

loves married man. Guy meets wife of married man and woos her
instead. When he arranges for the wife and mistress to meet, they
complicate matters further. It's a slow start and an overly dramatic
end, but everything in the middle is amazing. Awesome country
house with a swing and a lake. Joan Crawford is the mistress, and
the very charming Greer Garson plays the wife.

Nancy Kwan lets her hair down in *The World of Suzie Wong*, 1960.

royalty

What is a greater fantasy than being a princess? "No" followed by "thing." I thought we needed to devote some quality time to indulge this dream (per my shrink's orders). Because, you know, if you're gonna deprive yourself of something, it's just gonna come back and bite you in the ass later. That's free advice from me to you. So, put on these movies and eat that chocolate cake—all of it—you heard me. Do it now! No one's looking!

With the exception of baldy and Bergman on the next page, these rentals are all super-cheerful romantic stories.

And I asked: it turns out it *is* healthy to wear your drugstore tiara as much as you think you need to. Word to the wise though, just don't forget to take it off before you go to work—I learned the hard way.

Audrey Hepburn, the queen of twentieth-century cinema, in her debut in *Roman Holiday*, 1953.

Roman Holiday 1953.

Every little girl wants to be a princess, but this princess just wants to be a little girl. Audrey Hepburn's first movie. If all seventeen-year-old girls could be this stunning and poised, there'd probably be a lower teenage suicide rate. Audrey runs away from the palace to get a taste of real life. Gregory Peck (total BABE) is an American newspaperman in Rome on his way to being fired when he finds her asleep on a park bench. A wonderful way to see Rome—as if for the first time through the eyes of a princess. Ice cream, haircuts, and Vespa rides all look like much more fun than we know they actually are. A classic classic.

Anastasia 1956.

The old story of the lost Romanoff child. Ingrid Bergman won an Oscar for her heart-wrenching performance. Way on the dramatic side, it gets the tears flowing. Just a mention, this one's a smidgen different from the animated version. Yul Brynner is Ingrid's love interest, and Helen Hayes is awesome as the royal grandmother. Great rainy-day rental. Extra butter, please.

The Millionairess 1960.

Sophia Loren (perhaps the most stunning woman ever) and Peter Sellers star in this romantic comedy. She's a well-to-do Italian princess with money to burn. He plays an Indian doctor who has way too many principles and can't be bought. That's where the fun begins. I was just floored by Loren's wardrobe (especially the hats) by Pierre Balmain. So genius!

Shall we dance? Ingrid Bergman takes lessons from Yul Brynner in *Anastasia*, 1956.

The Princess Comes Across 1936.

Carole Lombard keeps up an amazingly bad Swedish accent throughout most of this film. Posing as a princess aboard a luxury liner, Lombard gets all the publicity she's looking for—not a bad idea. Unfortunately, she and the very charming Fred MacMurray get caught in the middle of a murder mystery. He's the onboard "concertinist" (read: accordion player). William Frawley (*I Love Lucy's* Fred) is the cuddly sidekick, and Lombard works in some excellent fur cape action.

The Reluctant Debutante 1958. Between

great fifties Technicolor and the title of this film, you can't lose. Sandra Dee is a seventeen-year-old American visiting London for the summer. Her father, Rex Harrison, and stepmother, Lady Broadbent (the gorgeous Kay Kendall), meddle in her dating life and throw her a coming out ball (no, she's not gay). John "Sexy" Saxon is the bad boy turned Duke. Great gowns in this film; unfortunately, most are repeated throughout the party montage. Angela Lansbury is the gossipy cousin of Lady Broadbent. This is the ultimate princessy love story.

Hedda Hopper

This is a character of a woman you should know about.
She was an infamous gossip columnist and Hollywood icon.
She started out as an actress and went on to have many
cameo appearances. She was famous for her outrageous
collection of hats and for her ongoing feud with rival
gossiper Louella Parsons.

Jimmy Stewart, Cary Grant, and Katharine Hepburn are shocked by the surprise ending of *The Philadelphia Story*, 1940.

weddings

Your mother tells you that you might as well slap her face if you're going to let only your father walk you down the aisle; your future mother-in-law wants to serve pork at the rehearsal dinner to your kosher family; and the real butterflies that you specially ordered (as larvae) that were supposed to be set free after the ceremony die in the organza box carried by the flower girl, who ends up just dumping the box upside down and shaking them out (I couldn't make this up). Deep breath. *The day that dreams come true.* The princess fantasy, your happily ever after, it's all here. That plus some ever so slight family drama, band-schedule conflicts, and out-of-season flowers you had your heart set on. Don't get me wrong. I wouldn't have had it any other way—except maybe in a perfect world I would've wanted the band singer to actually show up. One thing that has remained the same decade after decade is the mishegaas of a wedding. L'chaim!

The Philadelphia Story 1940. A top five favorite

of mine. Katharine Hepburn is the ultimate woman: rich, beautiful, and savvy. She makes the mistake of finding herself while preparing for her second wedding. Jimmy Stewart and Ruth Hussey are the tabloid photographer and reporter while Cary Grant charms everyone as Hepburn's first husband. Great witty retorts. (And don't miss *High Society*, the musical version with Grace Kelly, Bing Crosby, and Frank Sinatra, 1956.)

Royal Wedding 1951. The famous dancing on the

ceiling scene with Fred Astaire is just as good every time I see it. Jane Powell plays his heartbreaker of a sister, the dimpled-pixie type. Their singing and dancing team brings them to London to perform during the time of a . . . royal wedding. Fun scenes with Keenan Wynn playing his own twin brother. One American, one English, they have a communication breakdown between "Pip now" and "Dig you." Peter Lawford is Jane's down-to-earth, "royally" cute boyfriend.

Double Wedding 1937. Ignore the stupid title

because this is worthy of something a bit more clever. Myrna Loy and William Powell (remember the *Thin Man* series?) play opposites who, in a roundabout way, attract. A complex plot that's got a wonderful, if not obvious, climax. He walks around town in a full-length raccoon coat while she shows up in one gorgeous suit after another. A laugh-out-loud ending that's too silly not to enjoy. As always, their chemistry works wonders on the silver (or TV) screen.

Father of the Bride

1950. Forget you ever saw the remake (except Steve Martin *is* great). In this original, Spencer Tracy is a kind-hearted man, and his daughter, Elizabeth Taylor, drives him through the craziness that is her wedding. A touching story through dad's eyes about the feelings a man goes through when his baby grows up. Mom Joan Bennett (sister to actress Constance Bennett from *Topper*, see MAGIC) is the lovely all-American stereotype of a fifties housewife.

stacks of boxes

I see this phenomenon of packaging all the time in these movies (*The Palm Beach Story* is my favorite example). When I shop, yes, I admit, I'm driven mostly by my mission to acquire new clothes. I always leave with a bag or two. But where do I have to go in order to walk out with a mile high stack of neatly wrapped matching boxes in all shapes and sizes (which are then piled into the trunk by my chauffeur)?

dramarama

No matter how organized and in control your life seems to be, you can't escape a little drama. The sink stops up, you're fighting with your brother, your boss is a loser. All It Girls live with drama; it's what makes us human plus it's good for attention some of the time (OK, most of the time). These films are more on the soap opera side of drama, and that's what makes them great. They're overacted, overemotional, and all around overdone. Some of these even fall into the category of camp. Because the subject matter is almost always sex—and because today we have looser rules regarding the sideways salsa—they seem really funny, sad, even heart wrenching, but mostly funny (although no side-splitting laughs in *Splendor in the Grass*). Note the use of the word "place" in a few of these titles. Why? Look, if I knew, I'd let you in on it.

Sandra Dee cozies up to Troy Donahue in *A Summer Place*, 1959.

Montgomery Clift closes deals while Elizabeth Taylor waits for his attention in
A Place in the Sun, 1951.

A Summer Place 1959. I've never seen more drama

in my life. Troy Donahue and Sandra Dee are in love, confused, and scared. This is probably because her father is married to his mother, and her mother along with his father are nothing but trouble. It's like some ultra retro stepfamily saga, although *The Brady Bunch* was never like this. Troy's dorky monotone voice is made up for by his dreamy looks.

A Place in the Sun 1951. This is one of those

you've most likely seen in pieces on cable over the years. A mandatory film in the teenage drama genre. Elizabeth Taylor, Monty Clift, and Shelley Winters. Guess which one's his glamour girl and which one's his hidden lover with a secret? Clift is the country cousin just trying to make a place for himself (in the sun?). Taylor is the girl every guy wants and every girl wants to be.

Imitation of Life 1959. Isn't it too bad that one of

the few African-American stories I found was about a woman pretending she's not? Lana Turner is the lady of the house. Her African-American cleaning lady's daughter (Susan Kohner) passes for white and pretends that she's actually the daughter of the house. Sandra Dee, who plays Turner's *real* daughter, a perfect goody-goody (I know, it's so out of character), can't understand Kohner's reason for lying. This one is a remake of the 1934 original.

Splendor in the Grass 1961. Natalie Wood is

a small-town girl in need of a heavy prescription for Prozac. Her
dark and confused life includes the love of Warren Beatty (screen
debut)—wouldn't that be enough to make any girl happy? This
Oscar-winning story is pretty damn depressing, but see it and you
get to admire Wood's perfect beauty.

Born to Be Bad 1950. For whatever reason, I always

think of Joan Fontaine as a victim, but in this doozy, she's far from
it. She's Christabel; even her name sounds mean and manipulative.
She plays her men against each other, and even though she's our
heroine, you find yourself waiting for her demise. It's a meaty drama
of a greedy girl's desire for love and money from two different men
at the same time.

Peyton Place 1957. Rape, lust, lies, class issues—no,

it's not Jerry Springer. Lana Turner leads a huge cast including
Hope Lange and Lorne Greene. This overly dramatic saga of a small
ordinary town was later made into the first TV soap opera. Turner
owns the local dress shop where the latest in women's fashion is
featured amidst a juicy and tension-filled court trial.

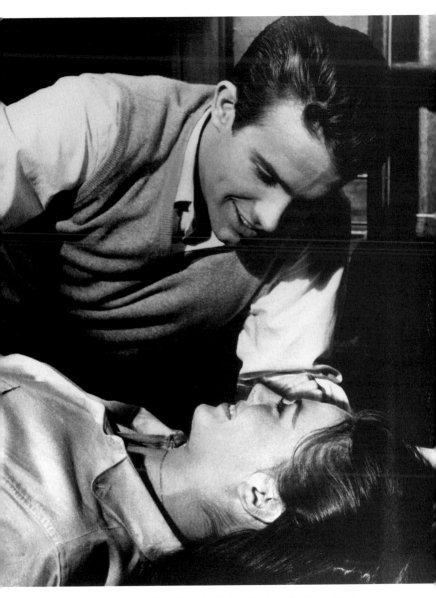

Natalie Wood falls hard for Warren Beatty in *Splendor in the Grass*, 1961.
(Wasn't he just in that pose with Vivien Leigh on page 72?)

musicals

Who doesn't want to see musicals? So they're unrealistic and silly but come on, aren't you curious what all that jumping around is about? Everyone likes music (some kind or another) and everyone likes movies (except my uncle Abe). Hollywood used to come up with some great combos of the two. Somewhere along the way the formula for a happy-go-lucky musical was lost. Today they really haven't mastered a way to make them work, with the exception of the animated stuff. Here's your chance to check out a lost art form. Consider it cultural, like going to the museum, only in your living room. Trust me. I'm sure you'll be entertained. And if you're not, what's the big loss? A few dollars at the rental place? Things could be worse.

Ginger Rogers and Fred Astaire cut the rug in *Top Hat*, 1935.

Top Hat

1935. Rogers and Astaire. Their dancing we've seen, but all the singing, romance, and sweet mistaken-identity story carries you through from beginning to end. Classic Irving Berlin songs, stunning clothes, and why can't I live in a world where men wear black tie every day? I guess that's why they call this picture *Top Hat* and not *The Gap*.

Singin' in the Rain

1952. Debbie Reynolds and Gene Kelly are actors, dancers, and singers in the time before "talkies." This super cheery love story is the quintessential musical that remains a favorite. And who doesn't know all the words to the song? How un-American.

Funny Face

1957. Really a must. Audrey Hepburn is a stubborn existential bookworm turned graceful model. Fred Astaire plays the Richard Avedon-inspired hep cat. The opening credit sequence along with in-film photos of Audrey are actually Avedon. Kay Thompson (author of *Eloise*, everyone's favorite brat) is a serious fashion editor who dictates what women want to wear. She's loosely based on Diana Vreeland, *Vogue*'s legendary editor. Gorgeous gowns! Super stylish photo shoots.

Donald O'Connor, Debbie Reynolds, and Gene Kelly break into song in *Singin' in the Rain*, 1952.

Viva Las Vegas

1964. How could we not have Elvis in this book? He's the über-stud race-car driver in Vegas, wearing a pompadour and singing to Ann-Margret. She shakes her booty in a way that only double-jointed girls can do. It's almost a spoof of itself. If this book were a class, this would be required watching.

The Wizard of Oz

1939. I can't imagine that you're not familiar with who's in this or what it's about. Just rent it—come on, you know you want to.

Mary Poppins

1964. I still don't understand. Is she an angel, a fairy godmother, or just a magical nanny? If you haven't seen this from start to finish in the last five years, do so now. Load up on "spoonfuls of sugar," turn out the lights, and don't pick up the phone. Julie Andrews can never be anyone else for me—I don't care how many times she puts on that *Victor/Victoria* costume. This is the golden age of Disney, and can you believe it's Andrews's first movie?! Oscars to her, music, and visual effects.

West Side Story

1961. Everyone knows this tragic musical. Romeo and Juliet in the mean streets. Every once in a while you have to watch it and let yourself sing along with the songs you know you know. Maybe there's even something to learn from it. Wouldn't gang violence today have a whole new twist if singing and dancing were involved? Best picture winner.

"making love"

Dictionary check. I know you've heard this expression, but before you get cocky, let me clarify. I wouldn't want to upset your delicate sensibility when you hear this used lightly and often. In "old moviespeak" it means simply and lamely . . . flirting.

Hollywood couples

In Hollywood there have been more than a few great mergers. Among the most famous are: Norma Shearer and Irving Thalberg; Katharine Hepburn and Spencer Tracy; Mary Pickford and Douglas Fairbanks; Lucille Ball and Desi Arnaz; Marion Davies and Charlie Chaplin; Lauren Bacall and Humphrey Bogart; Carole Lombard and Clark Gable; Betsy Drake (luck out) and Cary Grant; Jane Wyman and Ronald Reagan; Dolores Del Rio and Orson Welles; Audrey Hepburn and Mel Ferrer; and the one still going strong . . . Joanne Woodward and Paul Newman!

girl behind the guy

It's no news flash that women are the stronger sex.
I'm not burning my bra here, but let's come clean.
We have the babies, we do the job thing *and* the
home thing, and although sometimes it doesn't feel
like it, we do choose who we want to be with. So
here I've grouped together some rentals that show
us as Xena coming to the aid of girlie man in distress.
These babes all have a job to do, and in all cases
it's helping HIM! None of them even use the magic
wristbands or golden lasso. Just in case you think
their hard work might go unnoticed, at the risk
of giving anything away, I don't think these Warrior
Princesses are going home alone. With the exception
of *Mr. Smith*, the rest of these are fun frivolous films.
And even Señor Smitty himself is fun but only in that
kind of, but not really, serious way.

Cary Grant and Rosalind Russell can't seem to let each other go in *His Girl
Friday*, 1940.

Jean Arthur wears the pants (not literally) as Jimmy Stewart's secretary in *Mr. Smith Goes to Washington*, 1939.

His Girl Friday

1940. Trying to say good-bye to your ex-husband isn't easy, and why would you want to if he were Cary Grant? But when you're Rosalind Russell in the middle of a newsroom during a major scoop, things get out of control. Grant is the paper's editor and Russell is his top writer. Quick retorts and story twists make it chock full of fun, in addition to being a classic.

Mr. Smith Goes to Washington

1939. This isn't a female-driven film, but as the tough, seen-it-all secretary who loses her pessimism, Jean Arthur is so cool as the woman behind the man. Jimmy Stewart tries to make a difference as a scout leader voted senator. A feel-good movie that's a tad on the long side. The world's greatest underdog story from American favorite Frank Capra.

Paris—When It Sizzles

1964. Movies within a movie. Some people might say this takes you out of the story but in this case, it just keeps you more entertained. Audrey Hepburn is a secretary to William Holden's screenwriter. (He couldn't be sexier if he tried!) Under a tight deadline, together they write a movie while acting it out in fantasy sequences.

Let's Make Love

1960. This is a fun musical with Marilyn Monroe as the sweater-knitting, book-learning showgirl. She stars in a show that spoofs European playboy Yves Montand. So curious is he, that he comes to check out the rehearsal and lands the lead as himself! His true identity unknown, he romances Marilyn. Cameos by Milton Berle, Bing Crosby, and Gene Kelly.

career girls

Due to the nature of the beast, chicks in years past were primarily concerned with getting hitched and having a family. Then sometime (I'm not sure of the date—call Gloria Steinem) we started having jobs that we wanted to do, not just *had* to do, hence the birth of the career woman. So even though this book is proudly wall-to-wall romance and packed with dreamy guys, here's a fatty of a chapter dedicated to us—the working girls. And remember that your job doesn't define who you are, only what you *do*. I just thought a reminder never hurts when you're repeatedly hitting that snooze button every morning. Unless, of course, you happen to love your job, in which case the last statement doesn't apply—you'll just have to try to live with yourself.

Gorgeous Greta Garbo gleams in this publicity shot from the 1930s.

Ninotchka 1939.

There's nothing better then Greta Garbo making fun of Greta Garbo. Believe it or not, this is a comedy—the laughing kind. In Paris on official Soviet business, the bureaucratic and businesslike Garbo meets the enemy, Melvyn Douglas. She learns from him, simply for informative reasons, how to be a lady.

Pillow Talk 1959.

Oscar-winning screenplay for a story of two people sharing a party line. Doris Day and Rock Hudson are these enemies. The good part is that they only know one another by voice so when Rock finds out who she is, he romances her with a fake Texan accent. Day has the perfect It Girl occupation as an interior decorator. Tony Randall is the neurotic mutual friend. The best of the Hudson/Day collaborations.

They All Kissed the Bride 1942.

This title has almost nothing to do with this film. Joan Crawford is the high-powered executive of her family's trucking company, which is about to be exploited in a tell-all book. Melvyn Douglas, the book's investigative reporter, goes in for a closer angle. Crawford's unexpectedly weak knees and his forceful charm work quite well together. A flash of *Mommie Dearest* can't help but creep into your memory when you see Crawford behind a large desk barking orders.

Doris Day models her real 100 percent silk stockings in *Pillow Talk*, 1959.

Tony Curtis and Natalie Wood have the same taste in books in *Sex and the Single Girl*, 1964.

Sex and the Single Girl 1964. Another tale of

someone pretending to be someone else in order to get something
from someone (wait, stay with me). Tony Curtis is the editor of a
tabloid magazine, and he wants the dirt on Natalie Wood. She's a
famous shrink. Curtis pretends to be her patient and the story
begins. Wood is adorable while Lauren Bacall and Henry Fonda are
the great subplot couple. This film picked up the title of a real book
written by Helen Gurley Brown, editor of *Cosmopolitan*, in 1962.
Natalie Wood plays "Dr. Helen Brown," but other than that, there's
no real connection to the existing book.

Artists and Models 1955. If you can sit through

Jerry Lewis and Dean Martin, which by the way I can (don't hold
it against me), this is the original *Chasing Amy* without a lesbian.
A female cartoonist and her model roommate, Shirley MacLaine
(who's so cute with her pixie hair), live in the same building with
the two bachelors in search of jobs. Great Technicolor clothes
and sets.

Woman of the Year 1942. If you want to be OK

with being an underachiever (and who doesn't), this is a feel-good
film for you. Katharine Hepburn and Spencer Tracy. She's the
woman of the year and he's (surprise) a newspaper sportswriter.
Sweet romantic moments (except he does seem a little old for her),
and she's awesome at working the flirt (I took notes). How come
smoking looks so much cooler than it really is?

The Best of Everything 1959. Joan Crawford

runs the New York publishing world. Hope Lange is the young up-and-comer who wants her job, but not her loveless life. Hope's two roommates are women seeking careers and men in the big scary city. Dramatic and complicated love interests plus a dash of Louis Jourdan to give it some spice.

It Should Happen to You 1954. "Introducing

Jack Lemmon" makes this one worth it already. Judy Holliday is a New York girl who just wants to make a name for herself. After working as a girdle model, she decides to rent a billboard and paint her name on it. This causes a lot of trouble and excitement when (shocker) she becomes famous. She gets all she ever wanted at the expense of her relationship with Jack, the idealistic documentarian who wants to take her home to mom.

The Devil and Miss Jones 1941. Someone

told me this was a porno flick until I checked into it and found that that was *The Devil IN Miss Jones*. Don't make the same mistake. This is a (forgive the corny word) delightful movie about a tyrannical storeowner (Charles Coburn) who poses as an entry-level salesman to investigate an employee uproar. He's taken under the wing of Miss Jones (Jean Arthur), who turns out to be one of the trouble-makers (I know, you didn't see it coming). A TOTAL feel good.

Hope Lange gets "reviewed" by her boss, Brian Aherne, in *The Best of Everything*, 1959.

index of movies

index of selected actresses

movies on laser disk and dvd

At the time of print these were the movies available in the higher-quality formats of Laser Disk and Digital Video Disk. These formats often include bonus footage and trivia, including the original trailers. Check your local video store for updated lists of movies available in these formats.

Laser Disk:

Affair to Remember, An

After the Thin Man

Anastasia

Apartment, The

Auntie Mame

Awful Truth, The

Barefoot in the Park

Bell, Book and Candle

Blithe Spirit

Breakfast at Tiffany's

Bringing Up Baby

Casablanca

Children's Hour, The

Dark Victory

Designing Woman

Dial M for Murder

Father of the Bride

Funny Face

Grass Is Greener, The

High Society

His Girl Friday

Holiday

How to Steal a Million

It Happened One Night

Mary Poppins

Mildred Pierce

Mr. Smith Goes to Washington

Ninotchka

Nothing Sacred

Palm Beach Story, The

Peyton Place

Philadelphia Story, The

Place in the Sun, A

Please Don't Eat the Daisies

Reluctant Debutante, The

Roman Holiday

Sabrina

Sex and the Single Girl

Shadow of a Doubt

Singin' in the Rain

Some Like It Hot

Splendor in the Grass

Summer Place, A

Suspicion

That Touch of Mink

Three Smart Girls

To Catch a Thief

Top Hat

Viva Las Vegas

West Side Story

When Ladies Meet

Will Success Spoil Rock Hunter?

Wizard of Oz ,The

Woman of the Year

World of Suzie Wong, The

Digital Video Disk:

Ball of Fire

Bishop's Wife, The

Blithe Spirit

Casablanca

Dark Victory

Mary Poppins

Nothing Sacred

Philadelphia Story, The

Pillow Talk

Royal Wedding

Singin' in the Rain

Viva Las Vegas

West Side Story

Wizard of Oz, The

Woman of the Year

remakes and originals

Some of the films listed in this book have been made into TV movies, TV series, musicals, and plays. This list shows only the film version remakes. By the same token, some were also created from plays, musicals, and books—again, we're just stickin' with the films. This is a *video guide*, remember?

Affair to Remember, An (1957)
Original: Love Affair (1939)
Love Affair (1994)

Anastasia (1956)
Anastasia (1997) (animated)

Auntie Mame (1958)
Mame (1974)

Awful Truth, The (1937)
Original: The Awful Truth (1925, 1929)
Let's Do It Again (1953)

Ball of Fire (1941)
A Song Is Born (1948)

Bishop's Wife, The (1947)
The Preacher's Wife (1996)

Bluebeard's Eighth Wife (1938)
Original: Bluebeard's Eighth Wife (1923)

Born Yesterday (1950)
Born Yesterday (1993)

Bringing Up Baby (1938)
What's Up, Doc? (1972)

Children's Hour, The (1961)
Original: These Three (1936)

Dark Victory (1939)
The Stolen Hours (1963)

Dial M for Murder (1954)
A Perfect Murder (1998)

Father of the Bride (1950)
Father of the Bride (1991)

Gaslight (1944)
Original: Gaslight (1940)

His Girl Friday (1940)
Original: The Front Page (1931)
The Front Page (1974)
Switching Channels (1988)

Holiday (1938)
Original: Holiday (1930)

How to Marry a Millionaire (1953)
Original: The Greeks Had a Word for Them (1932)

Imitation of Life (1959)
Original: Imitation of Life (1934)

It Happened One Night (1934)
Eve Knew Her Apples (1945)
You Can't Run Away from It (1956)

Lady Eve, The (1941)
The Birds and the Bees (1956)

Midnight (1939)
Masquerade in Mexico (1945)

Mr. Smith Goes to Washington (1939)
Billy Jack Goes to Washington (1977)

My Man Godfrey (1957)
Original: My Man Godfrey (1936)

Ninotchka (1939)
Silk Stockings (1957)

Nothing Sacred (1937)
Living It Up (1954)

Philadelphia Story, The (1940)
High Society (1956)

Place in the Sun, A (1951)
Original: An American Tragedy (1931)

Sabrina (1954)
Sabrina (1995)

Shadow of a Doubt (1943)
Step Down to Terror (1958)

When Ladies Meet (1941)
Original: When Ladies Meet (1933)

Wizard of Oz, The (1939)
The Wiz (1978)

Women, The (1939)
The Opposite Sex (1956)